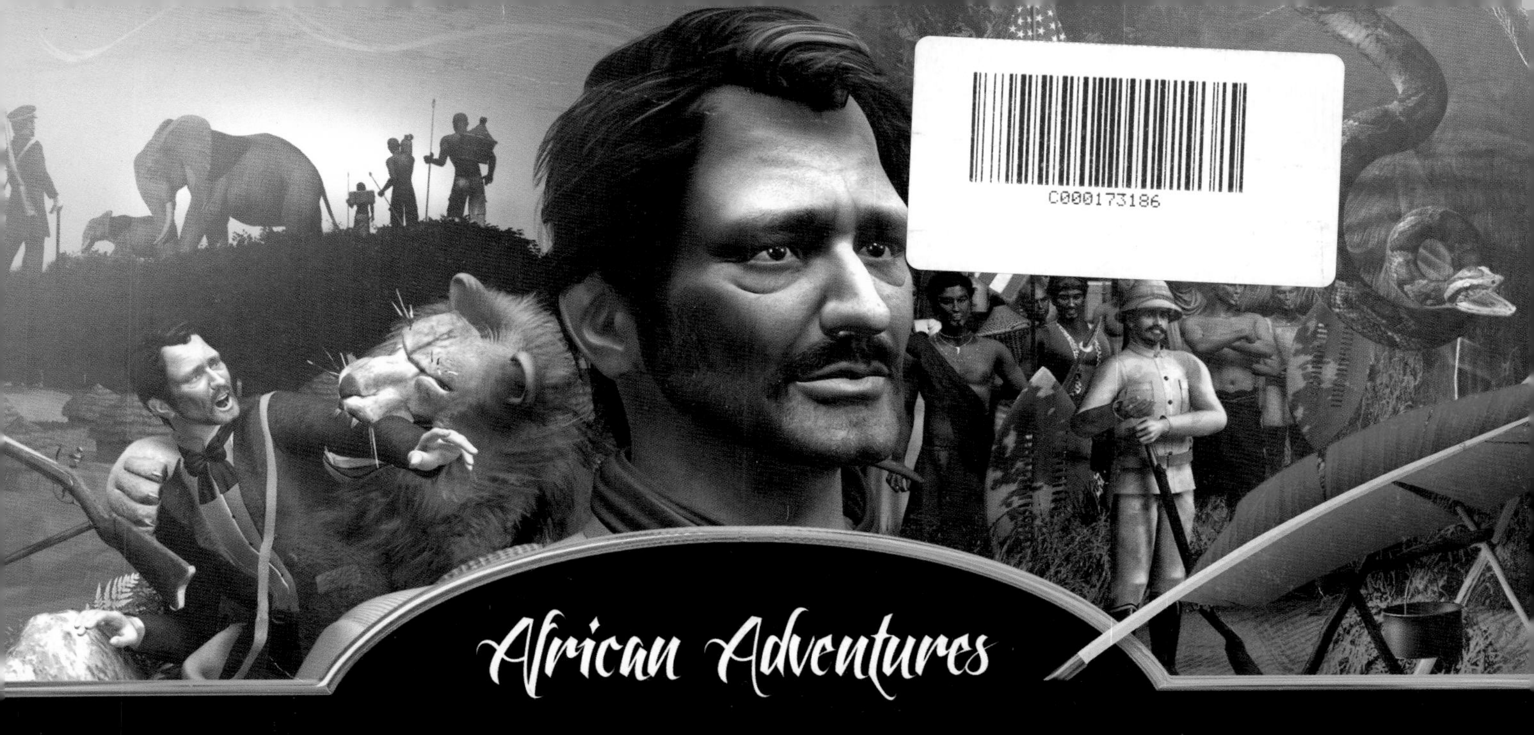

African Adventures

DAVID LIVINGSTONE

ARTWORK *by* GRAEME HEWITSON

STORY *by* MARGARET C. CHARLES

First printed 2013

ISBN 978-1-84625-399-7

Published by Day One Publications
Ryelands Road, Leominster, HR6 8NZ
TEL 01568 613 740 FAX 01568 611 473
Email: sales@dayone.co.uk
UK website: www.dayone.co.uk
USA website: www.dayonebookstore.com

Cover design and illustrations by Graeme Hewitson
Internal design and typesetting by Dave Hewer

Dedicated to all the children who attended the One Way Club at Bethel, Appledore, Devon during the 15 years it was operating. May you, like David Livingstone, be encouraged to give your lives to the service of the Lord Jesus Christ.

Margaret

Dedicated to my wonderful children, Josh, Aaron and Hannah.

Graeme

DAVID LIVINGSTONE

David was born on 19 March 1813 in Blantyre, a town in Scotland. He was the second of seven children. His parents were poor and life was hard. The whole family lived in one room, with no electricity and no heating. When they needed water – though they probably didn't wash much! – they carried it up several flights of stairs in buckets. They slept in two beds, the parents in one and all the children squashed into the other! As for food – imagine eating cold, sliced porridge every day. However, as Mr Livingstone was a tea salesman, there was one treat – cups of tea! But the God-fearing parents read the Bible, believed what it said and taught it to their children.

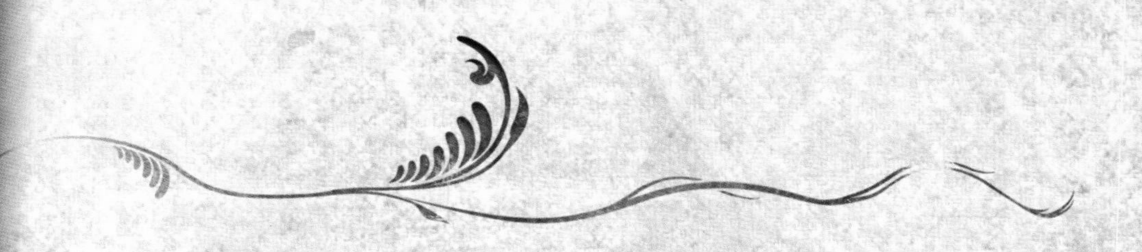

When David was ten, he started work in a cotton mill as a piecer. For six days a week he worked from six in the morning till eight at night, with a short break for breakfast and lunch. He found it very hard, as the air was full of cotton dust and it was so hot and extremely noisy. His job was to tie the broken threads on the spinning frame, so he had to crawl under machines, which was dangerous.

When he got home after work, he had to go to school until ten o'clock! But David loved learning – when he finished school he continued studying at home. He even had a book on his spinning frame at work!

Unlike many children, David enjoyed studying and couldn't wait until lessons began. His father encouraged him by teaching him to read, but his mother became angry at times because David would still be reading after midnight. "That boy … !" she would exclaim. With his first wage he bought a book to help him learn Latin!

The family attended church every Sunday and the children also went to Sunday School. When he was about sixteen he put his faith in the Lord Jesus and decided he wanted to spend his life telling other people about Him. Also on Sundays he and his father explored the countryside and this gave him a love of nature which stayed with him all his life.

Cranium
the skeleton of the head,
variously construed as including
all of the bones of the head except
the mandible, or as the eight
bones forming the vault lodging
the brain-cranial

David felt God wanted him to be a missionary. Many people thought a missionary should heal the sick as well as preach the Gospel, but how could he become a doctor? Then God gave him the opportunity – when just nineteen he was promoted to be a spinner at work, so he was paid more. Now he could save money so he could study medicine. But it was not easy – it took four years to save enough money to start evening classes at a College in Glasgow.

Later he moved to London where he qualified as a doctor. He loved Geography and as he was reading about different countries he imagined he was there preaching the Gospel. He couldn't wait to start!

Africa

In London, at a meeting about the slave trade, David heard the missionary Dr Robert Moffat, who was home from South Africa. As he was listening, David became so excited that he was sitting on the edge of his seat. Afterwards the two men met and he asked Dr Moffat, "Is there any work for me to do in Africa?" The great explorer looked at him and replied, "I have seen the smoke of a thousand villages where the Gospel has not yet been preached: go there." This was enough for David. God had spoken to his heart.

He rushed home to Scotland to say good bye to his family. His journey to Africa had begun.

Soon David was back in London and preparing to go. He took a ship for Cape Town, in South Africa. It took four months to get there; he spent the time reading books, especially the Bible, and telling the passengers about the Lord Jesus. The captain allowed him to preach to the sailors on Sundays.

One day he asked the captain, “How do you know where you are in the middle of the ocean?” He showed him an instrument used for finding an exact position – a quadrant – and taught him how to use it. David bought one and used it to make maps. This would prove to be very important later on. God was preparing him for his missionary travels. In March 1841 he arrived - Africa at last!

As soon as he could, he set off – his destination was Kuruman village where Dr. Moffat worked. First he sailed round the coast eastwards to Algoa Bay. Then he bought supplies, especially food, and hired guides, before setting off over land, heading north. Can you imagine a long, slow, journey – walking, or in a wagon pulled by oxen, for 700 miles! Each night they camped under a fantastic, star-studded sky – what a contrast to polluted London!

Eventually on 31 July 1841 they arrived. Not one to waste time, David immediately set about learning the language. What use was a doctor if he could not talk to his patients? And he so much wanted to tell the Africans of God's love.

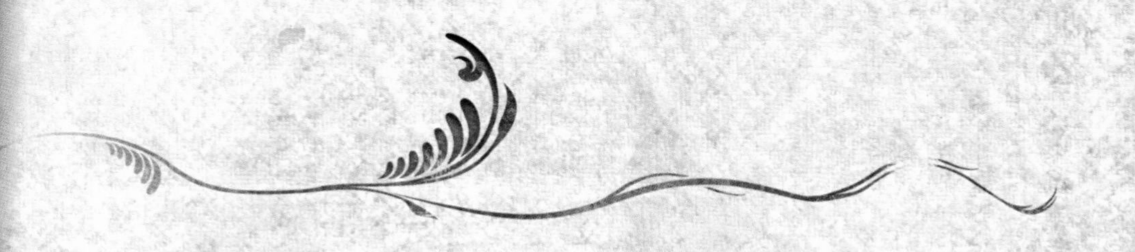

During his first year in Africa David travelled hundreds of miles on foot through dangerous, unexplored country. Since he was not tall, his helpers thought him weak, but as he kept marching on ahead, urging them to go faster, they changed their minds! They journeyed through areas where savage tribes lived, notorious for raiding the settlements of white people and killing men, women and children. But David continued. He was confident that God was with him and would protect him.

He came to the village of a very unfriendly tribe. The previous white visitors had been poisoned, but David ate their food and slept in their village. When the chief saw how trusting David was, he said, "We are friends."

In June 1843 David moved 200 miles north to a beautiful place called Mabotsa. He was looking for new headquarters. When he arrived, however, the villagers were very unfriendly. No one would help him to build a house. Nevertheless, this soon changed.

Lions were raiding the area. The villagers were terrified and in desperation appealed to David! "Can you help us shoot the great lion?" they cried. David and a teacher called Mebalwe went to an area outside the village where tribesmen had surrounded the lion. Mebalwe shot first – and missed! The lion was escaping through the ring of men. But David was a crack shot; he lifted his rifle, aimed, and fired. The villagers shouted jubilantly, "It's shot! It's dead!"

The villagers were both right and wrong: shot - yes, but dead – no! David was quickly reloading his gun, when out of nowhere the lion pounced and grabbed his left arm with its teeth. It shook him like a dog shakes a rat. Mebalwe aimed again, his gun misfired, but this caused the lion to turn on him, and it bit his leg. The tribesmen were fleeing in panic, but suddenly the lion dropped to the ground. This time the lion was dead! David's shot had wounded it fatally.

But David's injuries were serious. Imagine trying to mend an arm bitten by a lion – your own arm! It would never be the same again. Just as well he was right-handed!

While his arm was mending David returned to Kuruman to see his friends, the Moffats, who had returned from Britain with their daughter, Mary. Meeting her changed his life! Mary knew all about life in Africa as she had lived there since she was four. She listened to his stories and nursed his wounds. The more he watched her the more he thought, "What an excellent wife she would be for a missionary." He was falling in love. He plucked up courage to propose, romantically, under an almond tree. Mary gladly accepted.

They spent their honeymoon travelling back to Mabotsa in a bullock wagon! Upon arrival, Mary soon turned David's mud house into a home. A year later, baby Robert was born.

Another year passed and a daughter was born, Agnes. The family of four now moved north to Kolobeng. David soon took the opportunity to tell the people the Gospel and he had hardly finished his first message when the chief, Sechele, said, "May I ask some questions?" "Of course," replied David. As Sechele heard about salvation in the Lord Jesus through His death upon the cross, he believed. The Livingstones were delighted because here was an important man who realised he was a sinner who needed God's forgiveness.

The chief was later baptised in front of his tribe, and this encouraged them even more: they felt that what they were doing was right and being blessed by God.

Sechele invited the Livingstones to stay in Kolobeng. They had to build a new home – but by now they were getting used to it! Could you think of living in a mud hut in a remote village in Africa – and no TV or mobile? But this was God's plan for their life.

It was very busy: each morning they arose at sunrise, had family prayers and breakfast. Mary ran a school for the infants, as well as looking after their new baby, Thomas. David did manual jobs, such as ploughing, with animals of course. He also taught the villagers. Each night they met for prayer in the chief's hut, followed by milking the cows, then bed! They lived here for five years.

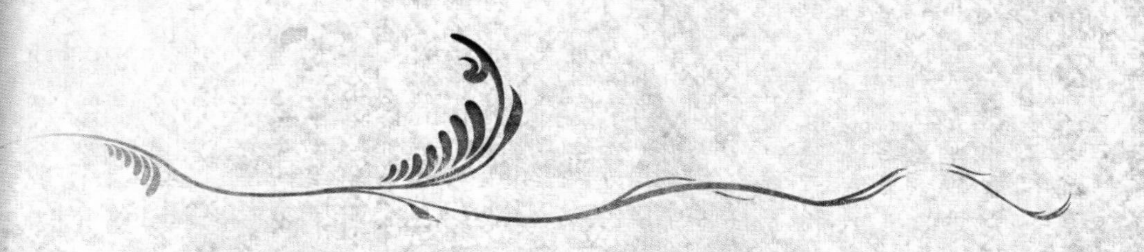

One day Chief Sechele had a good idea, so he thought! He wanted all his tribe to trust in Jesus as he had done, so he made a suggestion to Dr Livingstone, "I will have them all whipped until they become Christians."

Of course, David did not agree. Trusting the Lord Jesus is an individual choice and people cannot be forced. The chief reluctantly agreed that David could explain to all the tribe at once how to become a Christian, but he didn't think it would work. The only way he had ever got them to do anything was by beating them!

David preached, the people listened very carefully and every villager decided individually to trust the Lord Jesus.

When anyone was ill or injured, people said, "Go to the white doctor." People walked hundreds of miles to be cured. When he was operating they were very brave. They just stood and chatted to him! And of course he told them about the Christian faith. At this time he also spent a lot of time exploring areas of Africa where no European had ever been. His quadrant became very useful for making maps of his travels.

One day a stranger arrived with a message from his chief, Sebituane, "Please come to our tribe." It was a difficult journey through the Kalahari Desert, but David did not easily give up and so the two of them met.

He returned to his family, told his wife about the invitation and soon they set off. “How exciting!” exclaimed the children, as they travelled through the desert; they enjoyed camping under the stars and spotting wildlife in the daytime. But then problems arose: their guide lost his way and they nearly died from lack of water; then Mary gave birth to a girl, Elizabeth, but sadly she only lived for six weeks. Eventually they arrived and a year later another child was born, William.

David, however, realized he could not continue his work with four young children. His wife and family would have to return to the UK. There were tears as they boarded the boat and waved farewell at Cape Town.

Dr Livingstone wanted to find a route to bring trade to the centre of Africa from the Atlantic coast; it would help the poor people. Knowing his family was now safe, he set off on a great journey of exploration – by canoe. Can you imagine travelling in a dug-out canoe on a huge and dangerous river! This is what he did.

In November 1853 he travelled along the Zambezi River, over 1610 kilometres long, 450 metres wide, and full of danger, especially from crocodiles and hippos. But he was a determined and brave man, trusting in God. He visited villages along the river and was distressed when he saw slaves. He felt God wanted him to help abolish the slave trade.

"Mosi-da-Tunya, Mosi-da-Tunya," the people kept repeating. "Yes, I will go to see 'the Smoke that Thunders,'" Livingstone replied. Off he went with some African natives who lived inland, not really knowing where he was going, but knowing who was with him, for he believed in Jesus' promise 'I am with you always.'

For ten days they travelled, until he heard a great roaring sound – "This must be it." Then he saw it – a most spectacular sight – a roaring, foaming waterfall 120 metres high and more than half a kilometre wide. It is one of the world's natural wonders and he was the first white man to see it! He named it 'Victoria Falls' in honour of the Queen of Great Britain.

VINGSTONE.
N° 2

One day while trekking through the jungle his eye caught something on the ground. He bent down, picked up some stones and looked at them carefully, before casually throwing them away. A few days later one of the white men travelling with him asked him, "What were those stones you were looking at the other day?" "Diamonds," he simply replied. The man was shocked – throwing away diamonds! "Why did you do that?" David Livingstone replied, "I do not want the simple life here spoiled by hordes of prospectors." He enjoyed Africa as it was – very peaceful. He also believed that having Jesus Christ as his Lord was worth far more than all the world's wealth.

TYPVS ORBIS TERRARVM
OMNIS, TOTIVSQVE MVNDI NOTA SIT MAGNITVDO.

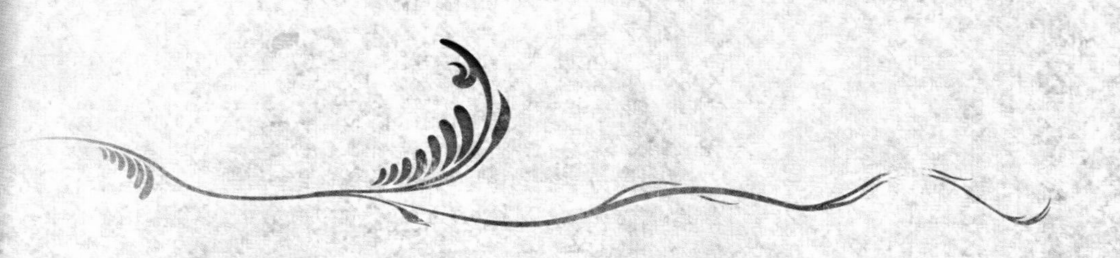

At last, Dr Livingstone reached his goal – Quilimane, a port on the Indian Ocean. He had crossed from coast to coast. When he arrived he was ill with malaria and the British Navy had to take him to Mauritius to recover so he could travel back to Britain. He hadn't been home for 16 years!

What a difference when he arrived back – he was famous! Everyone wanted to see the great explorer! He was given several honours and invited to meet Queen Victoria. The government gave him a grant of £5,000 for further expeditions and made him the British Consul at Quilimane with a salary. He now had money to plan better expeditions. He couldn't wait to get back!

In March 1858 the Livingstones arrived in Africa to start their great Zambezi expedition, to see if the river was navigable to the source. Dr Livingstone had to go on without his wife as they discovered she was going to have another baby. One day his party met a dreadful sight – a group of armed traders with a convoy of chained slaves. He was horrified and set free 84 slaves. As you can imagine he became the enemy of the traders.

Overall the trip was a disaster. The river had too many sand banks, rapids and waterfalls for big boats. After a few years his wife joined him, but she caught a fever and died three months later. With great sadness, he buried her under a baobab tree. He then sat down to write to each of his children, saying their mother was now in 'her eternal home, heaven.'

Dr Livingstone returned to Britain. He loved playing with his children and enjoyed meeting six year old Anna Mary for the first time. However, the time to leave and return to Africa came quickly. His new project was to find the source of the River Nile.

He travelled through dense jungle with his friends, Susi and Chuma. Imagine trudging through thick black mud and deep floods: he became very ill. Then his medicine ran out. But he still had his Bible which he read daily. "Where is he?" people asked in the UK and USA. No one knew – you could not ring him up! An American news reporter, Henry Stanley, was sent by his editor to see if he was dead or alive.

"Dr Livingstone I presume?" David Livingstone staggered out of the hut where he was living. "Yes," he said, just managing to raise his hat.

Dr Livingstone was alive, but only just. Susi had come running to him with the news, "An Englishman, I see him!" What greeted Dr Livingstone was an American flag and Henry Stanley! Stanley gave him letters from his family. He also shared his clothes, food and medicines and stayed for four months. He was very impressed with Dr Livingstone, especially his deep faith in God. He tried to persuade David to return home with him, but he said, "I still have work to do." Stanley journeyed home to tell the world that Dr Livingstone was alive!

"It is not all pleasure, this expedition," he said, as he and his companions carried on trying to find the source of the Nile. It certainly wasn't, but David Livingstone was not the kind of man to give up. He was nearly sixty years old and very ill from trudging through sweltering marshes and the relentless rain. His strength was almost gone. So his faithful workers made a hammock and carried him.

On his sixtieth birthday he prayed to God a prayer which started like this, "My Jesus, my King, my Life, my All. Once more I dedicate my whole self to Thee." Even after all his difficulties he still had the same devotion to the Lord Jesus.

On 27 April 1873 David Livingstone's faithful companions built a hut for him because he was not able to be moved. He wanted to press on but he was too weak.

A few days later, on the night of 1 May, he struggled out of bed to kneel to pray. A boy was watching him talking to his Master with his head in his hands. They found him the next morning still in that position. He had gone to be with the Lord he had served. Susi and Chuma decided his body should be taken to his homeland, but they buried his heart under a tree before setting off on the 2500 kilometres journey across Africa. It took nine months!

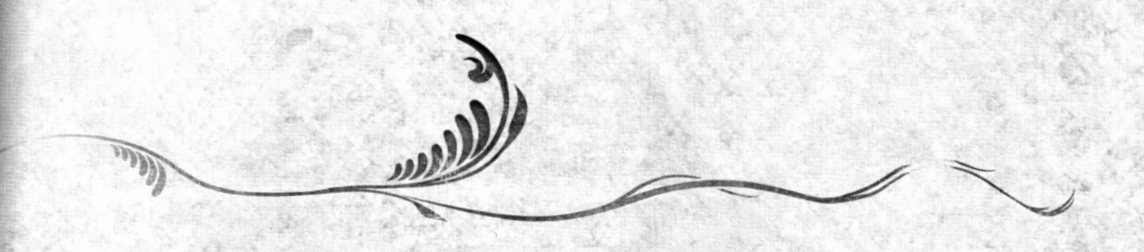

Dr Livingstone's friends carefully carried his body to the coast and Chuma accompanied it to Southampton. His body was taken to Westminster Abbey, London, where it was buried.

David Livingstone was a remarkable man who walked over 50 000 kilometres to explore the inner part of Africa, to meet the African people and to teach them about the love of God and His Son, Jesus Christ. His life of faith and devotion has inspired many young Christians to dedicate their lives to serve the Lord Jesus, both at home and abroad. Let us finish with some of his words:

"Nothing earthly will make me give up my work … I encourage myself in the Lord my God and go forward."

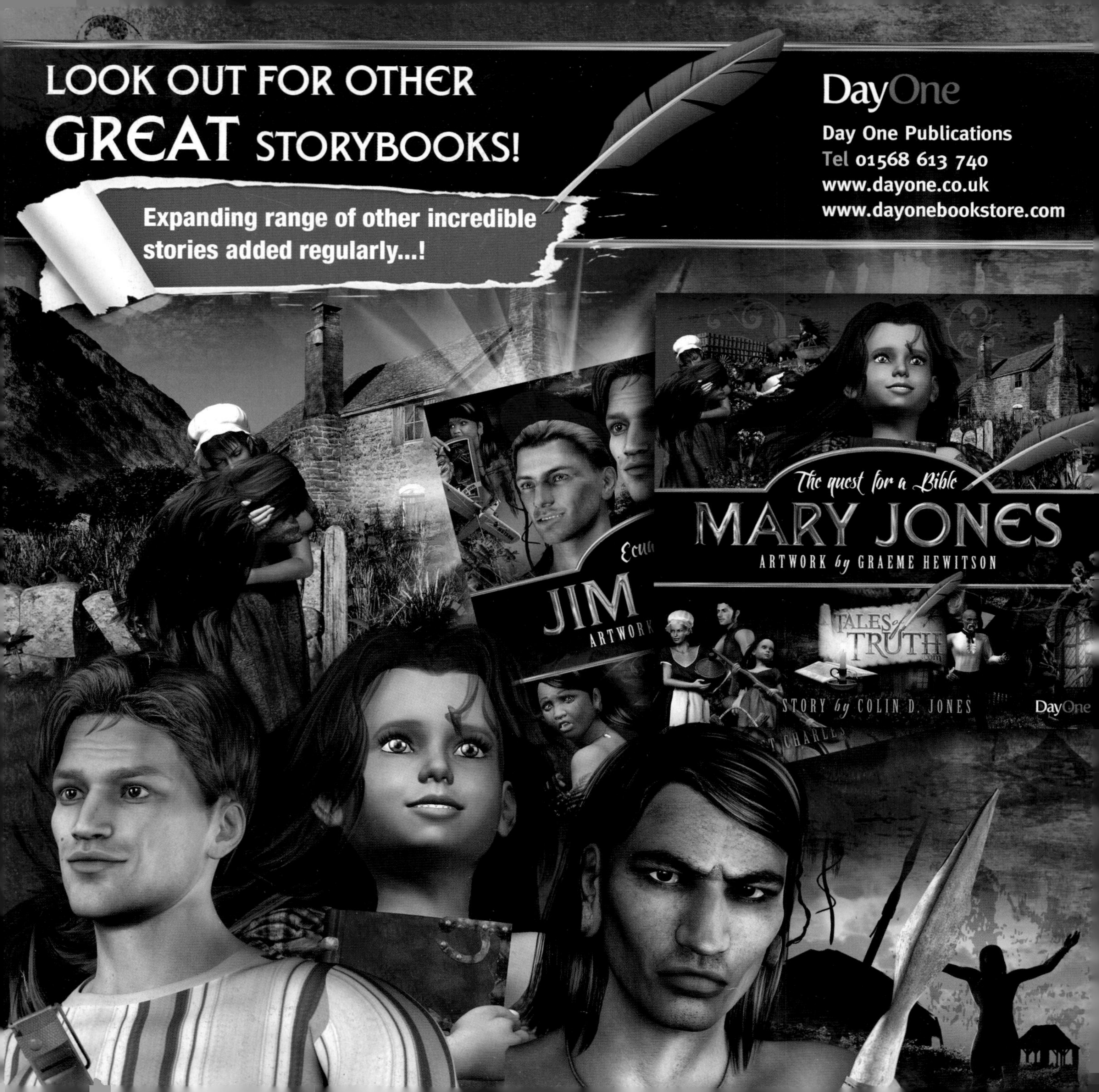
LOOK OUT FOR OTHER
GREAT STORYBOOKS!
Expanding range of other incredible stories added regularly...!
DayOne
Day One Publications
Tel 01568 613 740
www.dayone.co.uk
www.dayonebookstore.com
JIM
ARTWORK
The quest for a Bible
MARY JONES
ARTWORK by GRAEME HEWITSON
TALES of TRUTH .com
STORY by COLIN D. JONES
DayOne

Available to download now!
TELL THE STORY OF DAVID LIVINGSTONE TO A WIDER AUDIENCE!
TALES of TRUTH .com
The pictures in this book are available as powerpoint slides for teaching children at church or school!
David Livingstone
To be continued...
Teaching script and printable art page included!
MISSION FIELD ADVENTURES DAVID LIVINGSTONE
SERIAL STORY PART 1
DAVID LIVINGSTONE
Visit www.TALESofTRUTH.com
Purchase a STANDARD or ANIMATED powerpoint set, then simply download the incredible visual aids!
Helpful teaching pack and art page are included with each set.
"Kids are captivated by these resources!"